HOW TO
Be Jewish
IN
30 Seconds

BY RABBI KENNETH B. BLOCK
CARTOONS BY JOE SUTLIFF

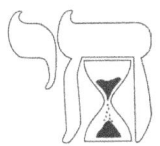

To everyone who challenged us to turn our
YouTube recordings into a book.
You taught me that discovering or
communicating with the One
is not complicated nor
does it require anything special.
The job of a Rabbi is to teach
and then get out of the way
so that the student can find their own path.

Table of Contents

FORWARD BY JENNY BLOCK, THE RABBI'S DAUGHTER

I AM THE RABBI'S DAUGHTER, as in the daughter of the Rabbi who wrote this book. My dad has a lot of amazing traits. He's smart, funny, kind, laid back, friendly, extremely well-educated. You get the idea. But perhaps his best trait is the fact that he always accepts people right where they are.

He acknowledges the fact that we are all different and yet, in the end, we all want the same thing—love and acceptance. We all want to feel happy and safe, and we all want to be treated with kindness and respect. And although the goal is the same, how we get there is different.

Nothing is too hard, according to my dad. It's all simply a matter of approach. But one thing is for sure, he always says, "If you don't go up to bat, you definitely won't hit a home run."

This life philosophy of his extends from everything from parenting to career success and from hobbies to, yes, religion. People are scared of religion. And to no surprise. It can be scary. Oft times it is scary. It can be daunting and untouchable. But it shouldn't be, because it isn't.

Religion is about faith. It's about belief. It's about finding peace. But above all else, it's about the believer.

If a religion involves gatekeeping, there's something wrong. Thirty Seconds to Being Jewish is not about opening the gate. It's about tearing the gate down.

There is nothing keeping you from practicing Judaism because you can practice however you like. The only wrong way is the way that doesn't feel authentic to you. This is within the realms of reality and honesty here. You can't say murdering a stranger on the street for no reason is how you're choosing to be Jewish. That's just stupid. Let's not do stupid.

I'm talking here about the ways and means you honor Judaism and its beliefs and traditions. I'm talking about candle lighting and keeping Kosher and building a Sukkot. This is one case where doing something, anything, is a thousand times better than doing nothing.

Better to say the blessing even if you don't have the wine. Better to sit outside under the stars even if you don't have a Sukkah. Better to take a moment at sunset on Saturday night and make plans for the week even if you don't have a spice box or a braided candle.

The only thing I know about anything is that my father is generally right, even when I wish he wasn't. Thirty Seconds to Being Jewish is 36 ways to go up to bat. Why 36? Because that's double Chai. Chai means life! And the letters that make up the word, chet and yud, stand for 8 and 10 respectively. So Chai is 18, making 36, you got it, double chai!

Here's the thing. This book is no pressure, just opportunity. We shouldn't turn away from Judaism because we can't do the all the things. We should turn to Judaism because we can do what we can do. And that, believe it or not, is enough.

Because in the end, being Jewish is about going up to bat and taking a swing at the one longing we all share— the finding of faith.

INTRODUCTION

I'M HERE TO TELL YA: you can be Jewish in 30 seconds or less.

Hear me out. Many of my colleagues, both Jewish and Gentile present their religions as all or nothing, insurmountable mountains of material. So, naturally, nearly everyone is going to shy away from it. Religion is like sailing. If you learn some of the basics, you can sail a boat. You're not going to be in the America's Cup or sail around the world, but you can love it anyway.

I think a disservice has been done to Judaism by presenting it as all or nothing—telling Jews what they can and cannot do and that you have to give up this and that. The only thing that this results in is people walking away. But it doesn't have to be that way. You can practice Judaism in just 30 seconds a week by picking a Jewish activity and, well, practicing it.

"Baruch ashem ..., and an extra one for the cherry on top."

1
COUNT YOUR BLESSINGS

RECITING A BLESSING takes less than 30 seconds. In
fact, you might even have time to recite two. The musical
"Fiddler On The Roof" made a joke out of a blessing
for the Czar. It was funny because there is a blessing for
virtually everything in Judaism. You don't have to learn
all the blessings, nor do you need to recite all of them. Just
start with a couple. The good news is that the majority of
them begin the same way:

BA-RUCH A-TAH A-DO-NOI
ELO-HAI-NU ME-LECH HA-O-LAM

In English you are saying, "Blessed are You, Lord and
King of the universe."

And when it is a blessing that fulfills a commandment
you add "who has commanded us to do X" which is just
a few more words. You can start by learning the blessing
over bread. Before you eat, add this to the above:

HA-MO-TZI LE-CHEM MIN HA-A-RETZ.

In English you are saying, Thank you, God, for bread.
Or technically, "Blessed are You, Lord and King of the
Universe, we thank you for our bread."

That's it! You don't have to do thousands of blessings.
You can decide to commit less than 30 seconds to this
practice. Perhaps you would like to add a second or a

third blessing, or maybe not. Reciting a blessing teaches us humility and helps us to recognize that we're not the center of the universe. Saying a blessing is a very Jewish thing to do because it recognizes and centers God.

You do not need to stand to do this blessing, bow a certain way, put on a hat, or do a little dance. Just be present for the 30 seconds it takes to say thank you. It's about acknowledging there is something greater than you, more important than you, and always present.

Among the myriad of blessings in Judaism there is one for when you see a rainbow, meet a king, acquire an item for the first time, or even when you see an ugly person. No need to look up the last one; here it is: "Blessed are You, Lord and King of the universe who creates people of unique appearance." There are many websites where you will find links that list various blessings.

So, you say the blessing and you eat. "Blessed are You God, King of the universe gives us food to eat, provides food for us, or who provides for us in the universe with farmers and people can grow food and transport it." You don't have to use the exact formula because there is no exact formula. Don't let anyone tell you that there is only one way to say a blessing. A blessing is your conversation with God. So, you are fulfilling the commandment of acknowledging that there is a God and that things come to us not of our own doing.

2
SAVOR SABBATH

CALLING THE FAMILY to have dinner together on Friday night takes less than 30 seconds. You can have a Shabbat dinner when the whole family sits down once a week, turns off the TV, the tablets and , the phones, says a few prayers, and talks with one another. It doesn't have to last for hours, and it doesn't require us to go anywhere.

When you look at the book of Genesis, specifically during the story of creation it says, "it was evening and morning: day one" "it was evening and morning, day

"No, going through the drive-thru does not count as a family meal."

two," etc. This gives us the definition of a day, which begins at sundown. I'd like to focus on not so much the day itself, but rather the sunset. Imagine it's Friday. The sun is setting. It is the beginning of the Sabbath. Even if you can't set aside the entire day, you all can set aside one evening meal once a week to get back in touch with each other. As the sun sets on Friday you light candles, and say a blessing, "Blessed are you Lord our God, king of the universe, who has commanded us to light the Sabbath lights." You turn off distractions—whatever they might be—and you acknowledge this as the time to get in touch with each other to feel the spirituality that each of us brings to the table.

And now you can begin the Sabbath meal.

Dinner can be elaborate, or simple. It could be home-cooked or takeout. That is not what's important. Don't ruin the moment with scrupulosity, or being picayune. What you are doing is setting aside time—this time and this meal—to be together as a family.

Who has the worst day or the best day? What happened to you today, this week? Perhaps you haven't had a chance to talk to each other all week, so for the next hour or two you're going to sit, you're going to eat, you're going to compare notes, and you are going to get in touch with each other without other requirements. You don't have to do anything, and you don't have to not do anything you put all that aside, because that is not what the Sabbath is about.

You are not landing a 747 or performing a coronary transplant. The Sabbath is about having a moment to be with the family to talk about what happened. Take this one moment to acknowledge God, family, and discuss the week.

It only takes 30 seconds to call the family to the table, light a candle, eat, and talk. That's it. I hope everyone enjoys their moment out of time on Friday night with a little peace and quiet with the family.

"I appreciate the piety, son, but you don't have to say the shema before you eat your mother's tuna casserole."

3
TA DAH! THE SHEMA

YOU CAN RECITE THE SHEMA IN LESS than 30 seconds, you can easily say it twice a day or more if you like. The Shema is sum total of all Jewish teachings and it belongs to all Jews. Recite the Shema and you have declared that you are Jewish. "Listen, Israel, I believe that God is One." All of the rituals you perform are reminders of this affirmation.

The Shema is a very important and easy phrase: "Shema Yisroal, Adonai eloyanu, Adonai echad." You are going to recite it at least once a day: once when you get up and once before you go to sleep, or just once in the middle of the day. There's no specific rule about when.

What's important is to verbalize the acknowledgement that you are Jewish. So you begin, "Hear O Israel," and the next word is God's personal name. In English you might sometimes say Yahyouh or Jehovah, but the Hebrew letters can not be pronounced so you are going to substitute the word "Adonai," which means lord or master. This is the most basic idea that Judaism teaches the world. Whenever you feel like connecting with the One, you say "Shema Yisroal, Adonai eloyanu, Adonai echad,"

So what do you get out of it? You may be sitting in

a room by yourself saying the Shema, but you are not alone. The Shema connects you to the One, and it helps you realize that you are interconnected with all that was and all that will be. This was the teaching of all the matriarchs and patriarchs. They wanted to convey to us that we are all part of the system. The universe is in you. You might be small but you're never alone. You are part of all creation and all creation is part of you. It's your past, present, and future. You are one star in the universe. If you want your star to shine, recite the Shema. Your light will shine because you acknowledge that everything is one.

4
MEZUZAH MEANING MAKING

HANG A MEZUZAH on the "doorposts" of your house.

Perhaps you have heard the word Mezuzah, or you've seen one. The word "mezuzah" is often used to refer to just the case. So, let's start off by saying that the Mezuzah has two parts: its case that protects the scroll that fits inside the case. Just putting up a case isn't enough. Although you can certainly collect Mezuzah cases and display them in your home. I have a neat collection myself.

Today you are going to put the Shema on the doorpost of your house. Why? That is what it says in the Torah: Put a Mezuzah on every door in your home so that whenever you enter and whenever you leave, whether from your home or from a room in your home, you're reminded once again that you are a part of everything.

You might be thinking, "This seems like a little more than 30 seconds worth of effort." Sure, you need to go out and find a Mezuzah, and then buy a kosher scroll that has the Shema written on it, and then you need to nail it up.

Stop overthinking it. God is not concerned whether the Shema inside is written on an animal skin, a piece of the papyrus, or a piece of paper. Put aside that you have to spend $100 on a kosher scroll written by a scribe. You

"Are you SURE the exact angle is described in Numbers?"

don't. Find the Shema in a Prayer Book and write it out, have a friend write it out, go online and search "Shema text" and print it out.

You could even stick the Shema in a mismatched piece of Tupperware and Duck Tape it to the doorpost? You certainly could. From an artist's point of view that would not be aesthetically pleasing. Since I am going to put the Shema on my door posts I would like the case to be pretty.

OK, now "No one expects the Spanish Inquisition," to quote Monty Python. "But Rabbi you're talking about making a declaration on your door saying this is a Jewish house!" With all the various deliveries that come to your front door, you might not want to make it visible. You are not obligated to make the Mezuzah visible.

The Rabbis address this very issue in the Talmud. If you feel that it is safe, then it goes on the outside. If you don't feel it's safe, put it inside so that only you can see it as you are coming and going.

A mezuzah for purchase is readily available online, as is a printed or handwritten copy of the Shema to place inside. Once you hang your mezuzah you will be reminded that "God is One."

5
ROCK THE TZEDAKAH

YOU CAN DO THE RIGHT THING in 30 seconds or less by making a tzedakah box. Judaism does not have a word for charity nor is there the concept of charity. Don't let the use of the word charity, when used in reference to Jewish institutions, mislead you. In general usage the word means supporting non-profit institutions and organizations but does not refer to a religious concept. However, as Jews we can focus on the religious idea of tzedakah:
"to do the right thing." The Hebrew prophets made it plain that you are expected to do the right thing with your money and possessions. And that means sharing what you have gained. It doesn't mean giving everything away, nor does it mean living an austere life. There are multiple ways and many opportunities to do the right thing. Focus on one easy, simple, and important way to do the right thing: Make a tzedakah box.

The Tzedakah box is the Jewish version of a "curse jar". Pick a container, jar, or box, and don't wait until you curse to put money in it, because you now have a tzedakah box. You can use a peanut butter jar, pickle jar, that Tupperware container with the mismatched lid, you can designate anything and write the word tzedakah on it which means I'm doing the right thing.

Put in any amount of loose change, coins, or paper. In a short time it will be time to decide where to send the money, for example, The American Cancer Society, the Alzheimer's Association, your local temple or even your local church. Consider your local food bank.

Your Tzedakah box sits in the kitchen, near the front door, or on a dresser. You are not limited to just one Tzedakah box; everyone in your family can have his or her own. The donated money does not need to go to the same place, and each member of your family can choose where to send the money they have collected.

The Tzedakah box collects loose change and perhaps a few bills. When you empty the box you can always supplement your contribution from your bank account. And don't overlook the fact that you have skills and talents that are worth sharing. Besides giving money you can do the right thing by volunteering your time.

The Tzedakah box does not require a prayer or a blessing or any rituals. The Hebrew prophets would be proud of you for giving. The prophets made it clear that being Jewish was not just about rituals, but rather about doing the right thing when the opportunity presents itself. So in 30 seconds or less, by giving Tzedakah you will have made the Hebrew prophets proud.

6
SERVE THE SILENCE

KEEPING QUIET, staying silent, and being civil doesn't even take a second, never mind 30 seconds. This is one of those things that makes being Jewish very unique in that it is both easy and hard. It is easy for you to see when other people gossip, spread rumors, or just make something up. It is hard because of the very human inclination to criticize other people, make comments about them, or tell others that they like to gossip. See how quickly you turn listening into gossiping about others! It happens without your thinking, your tongue is moving before engaging the brain. That is why this 30 seconds is called L'Shon HaRah or "guard your tongue from speaking evil."

The only way that I know to keep you from being a gossip is for you to sit in a boat in the middle of a lake all by yourself, inhabit a desert island without internet, or find a cave in the mountains with no mobile phone service! These are too extreme to be realistic, although they could certainly reduce the stress in your life. Even limiting contact with other people is not a reasonable solution to keep you from gossiping. Humans are social beings, being social means talking, and talking leads to gossip. This 30 seconds sounds like it might be pretty tough, right?

"Mabel said that Frank said that Janice said that Holly said, but you didn't hear it from me..."

If you live in a lighthouse, isolated, and alone it would be really easy to put this into practice. But you don't live in isolation, so what are you to do? Start by looking at the word, L'Shon means tongue and HaRah means evil, bad, or wicked. The goal here is to not to use your tongue to hurt other people, to promote false statements, or to spread rumors.

There's nothing wrong with putting things on Facebook, Mastodon, YouTube, Instagram, TikTok, Twitter/X, or any other social media. You went here, you went there, you went on vacation, etc. That's all informative, factual, and true. A social bulletin board informing us of what you did, where you went, and how your family is doing is a blessing, in fact.

The danger is when you pass along something you heard, you make something up, or you repeat something that has been proven not to be true. Because then it's out there. The analogy that the rabbis use in the Talmud is that gossip is like firing an arrow. Once it goes from the bow you can't control it, and you can't stop it. So even if you meant well, once it's out there it's going to be repeated and passed on. It could even be modified or edited in ways you never intended.

Before you share something, stop for 30 seconds and think to yourself: "am I spreading rumors or gossiping?"

When all else fails remember what Bubbies (grandmothers) all over the world have said: "if you can't say anything nice, don't say anything at all."

7
SUKKOT SIMCHA (JOY)

TO HONOR SUKKOT, all you need to do is enjoy a
Thanksgiving meal, say a prayer or blessing. There is no
formula or special words. If you start by listing the things
you are thankful for, others around the table will surely
join in. Enjoy family and food and be grateful. Criticizing,
debating, and complaining can wait for another holiday.
You are commanded to rejoice and be glad, so rejoice and
be glad!

You can observe the holiday of Sukkot without
building a booth, a Sukkah, a harvest booth. Now you
might say "what's Sukkot without a booth?" but the
holiday isn't about building structures, as much as it is
about thanking God for fruits, vegetables, your family,
friends, and the freedoms you enjoy. Nothing, however,
prevents you from building a sukkah as well!

You can thank the Puritans of New England in Boston
for being Old Testament-oriented. They decided to take
the Jewish holiday of Sukkot and make it into a festival.
What could be easier, a Thanksgiving meal when you
give thanks to God for your fruits and vegetables. This is
yet another holiday when we are commanded to overeat!

In the book of Leviticus we are instructed to take the
fruit of a goodly tree, branches of palm trees, boughs of

thick trees, and willows of the brook. Needless to say the scholars and Rabbis were off and running to dictate what the boughs of thick trees and the fruit of a goodly tree would be. They concluded that the "four species" described are a closed fond of the date palm tree, the boughs of myrtle and willow, and the fruit of a citron.

A citron is a large fragrant fruit with a thick rind resembling a rough lemon. The rabbis picked these because they are native to the biblical land of Israel. And this made sense to them since they wanted to duplicate what our ancestors did in Biblical days. And, of course, their opinion of what the quote from Scripture means has validity to you if you choose to follow their view. These items can be purchased online if you like.

For those living outside Israel, these plants may not familiar. We can honor any plants that need water and sun to grow. Is there a fruit on your table that is pleasant to look at and has a pleasing smell? Let everyone hold it, smell it, perhaps taste it, and then say something nice about it.

You may not have a palm, willow, or myrtle growing near you, but you probably have green plants that need water and sun. Put plants, branches, or leaves on the table and call everyone's attention to them. It only takes 30 seconds to acknowledge that we are dependent on plants.

8
WHEN MORRIS SPEAKS, LISTEN

JUST AS PINOCCHIO had Jimmy Cricket, Peter Pan had Tinkerbelle, and Homer Simson had angel Homer, we have Morris Ayin. Being Jewish in 30 seconds means listening to Morris. Think of Morris as your appearance advisor, your life coach, your own Jimmy Cricket. Morris will help you project the best image of yourself to help your best self shine outward. Pause for a moment, right now, and you will feel Morris' presence.

"Heads or tails?"   *"Probably."*

While the common expression is "don't judge a book by its cover," the reality is that you will be judged by how you appear to other people. And it's not just about people; you judge a restaurant by its ambiance, or its menu, or what your distant cousin said about the decor. You judge those around you by their clothes, shoes, or the brand on their hat. It is not an accident that publishers spend a considerable amount of money on the cover!

From now on stop when you're not sure what to wear, where to eat, what movie to watch, or book to read. Ask Morris for advice. This allows you to check in with yourself and make sure that the choices you are making are consistent with who you are. The way you act tells others who you are, and too often you aren't careful enough with Mar'it Eyin.

Mar'it means appearance and Eyin means eye. What do people conclude about you, based on what you wear? Dress appropriately for the occasion. Make sure your actions express the best of you. This way you are in control of what others think of you. You are your own role model. Like it or not, how you appear to others, Mar'it Eyin, is how you will be seen.

Morris will keep you from needing to apologize because you will be you.

9
THE PATH TO A HAPPY HOME

IN 30 SECONDS, you can choose to be happy instead of choosing to be right. Excessive human pride would have us choose to be right regardless of the situation, but it doesn't have to be this way. Happiness, serenity, and peace can be yours. You can begin by practicing Shalom Ha'Bayit, peace in your place of residence. Perhaps you've been practicing Shalom Ha'Bayit for a while without even realizing it. Now you are going to practice it intentionally.

You have a choice of how to respond when someone in your life says something disturbing, contrary to your views, or antagonizing. These situations happen all the time, so it is worthwhile to make Shalom Ha'Bayit part of your practice.

The word Bayit means home or house, but it can also be defined as where you live: a county, a state or commonwealth, a country, and a planet. You don't want to use Bayit in the narrow sense four walls and a roof. When you use Bayit to mean where you are, at that moment you are home.

So Shalom Ha'Bayit asks you to stop for a moment before you respond to what's going on around you, before you say something or criticize someone. Ask

"Option A, I blast you. Option B, you pummel me. Option C, we grab some lunch and discuss Rabbi Block's book."

yourself if you want Shalom Ha'Bayit, and if being right more important than being happy. Consider how the other person might respond to what you are going to say. Remember your goal is serenity, wholeness, completeness, and shalom.

Practicing shalom Ha'Bayit can be a challenge at family gatherings like Thanksgiving, Passover, Rosh Hashanah, or any time when the whole family is in one room, with the potential for arguing.

Rid yourself of the idea of winning or losing because it is not a constructive or helpful goal. Shalom Ha'Bayit will give you better results, a better product, and peaceful family gathering.

10
CHANUKAH OH CHANUKAH

MAKING LATKES AND LIGHTING CANDLES for
Chanukah are both easy and fun ways to be Jewish in
30 seconds. Decorating your home in blue and white
lights adds to the festival. Chanukah decorations abound
online and in stores and there is no way that you can
over decorate and minimize the holiday. Chanukah is a
holiday that celebrates religious freedom, so you decide
what is appropriate.

Yes, latkes are appropriate because they're cooked
in oil and the holiday celebrates oil and a miracle of
candle lighting in the oil lasting, but you know you can
go to McDonald's and pick up an order of fries. Or
better yet an order of hash browns, they look just like
latkes to me! They're cooked in oil too. Or how about
donuts, sufganiot, which are also cooked in oil. Wherever
you look Chanukah runs on Dunkin! There are lots of
things that could fit the bill. What's important is having
a nice celebration and not getting bogged down in
irrelevant details.

Since Chanukah is a post Biblical holiday, its
observance and customs have been added throughout the
centuries. So you can freely add your ideas to the holiday.

When it comes to lighting the Chanukah candles,

*"We take cash, checks, credit or chocolate gelt,
as long as it's not last year's."*

remember, they're candles! You don't need a special
Chanukah menorah or special Chanukah candles. You
can go to Yankee Candle, Walmart, Amazon, or anywhere
candles are sold. Since the holiday is celebrated for eight
days you're going to light a candle on the first day two
on the second and three on the third etc. until on the last
day all 8 are burning. Or you can start by lighting all 8
on the first night, 7 on the second night, 6 on the third
night etc. thus reducing a candle by one every day until

on the last night only one candle is lit.

The order in which you light candles or the order that they are placed in the menorah is not what's important. You're celebrating religious freedom, and the ability to worship Judaism and be Jewish and you do it by eating things cooked in oil. You do it by having family together and talking and playing games, spinning the dreidel giving presents lighting candles.

And you can't resist a good gambling game. What could be better, a holiday that requires you to gamble! You are going to gamble with a 4 sided top, a dreidel. Think of it as miniature roulette. Everyone antes up to play, and the rest is pure chance. Add to the pot, take half, take all, or pass, no skill or choice determines your fate.

Chanukah is a winter celebration, observed during the dark of the sun and the dark of the moon. You chase away the darkness with any kind of lights, you remember the oil used in the eternal light by eating any kind of fried foods, and you gamble the evening away. Most important, you get to spend time with your family and friends.

Have a happy, joyous Chanukah.

"What do you say, Lord? The five iron or the seven?"

11
KIBBITZING WITH GOD

PRAYER IS OFTEN DESCRIBED as a ladder. Picture a ladder that you would use to reach the books on the top shelf, to paint a tall wall, to hang a light fixture. You use it to reach upward to places that you cannot reach while standing on the ground. Prayer is the spiritual ladder you use to climb from the material world into the spiritual realm where God resides.

When the time comes to have a conversation with God, you can speak out loud or you can speak softly. You can shout, or sing. You can formulate the words in your mind. You can stand or sit. You can raise your hands or fold them if you like. Begin with the salutation of your choice. I like, "Hello, God. It's me."

Don't be misled about the nature of prayer. In some religions, in order to pray, you need to kneel, to cross yourself, or to face Mecca or Jerusalem. You have to speak in another tongue—Arabic, Hindi, Latin, Hebrew. All of these are valid forms of prayer. They are not, however, the only forms that prayer can take. Prayer is as simple as kibbitzing with God.

Our individual conversations with God have become organized into worship, which naturally applies rules that tend to be the opposite of an organic conversation.

When prayers require rules, a book, an order, a formal or a unique language, or a doxology, if you want to be a participant, you are required to follow their rules. And if you don't follow the rules, some religious authority will correct you and show you how it is to be done. This makes perfect sense if you are going to participate in a group. It is not, however, the only way that you can have a conversation with God.

Prayer is a conversation with God. No rules required. You can have a conversation with God. Abraham, Isaac, and Jacob did. Moses, Rebecca, Leah, and Sarah did, Mohamed did, Gandhi did. All the world's spiritual and religious heroes have had conversations with God. And most of them either created or attended worship services. What's more: they separated the two, and so can you.

Why not put aside the rules that someone convinced you were needed in order to pray, any of the body motions that someone told you were required, and the myth that God only understands a certain language and, instead, just have a conversation with God whenever you want to, however you want to. You will be joining the ranks of all of your Biblical, spiritual, and religious heroes who kibbitzed with God. It's just a very simple, easy communication and it is very, very Jewish.

12
SAY GOODBYE

SAY GOODBYE TO THE SABBATH at Havdalah. Havdalah is the end of Shabbat, the time that prepares you for the week ahead as opposed to the Shabbat, which prepares you for the day of rest. So, what's the difference? Why do you need two nights in a row? Couldn't you just do them both on the same evening?

Every sport has a huddle before every game, whether it's a team sport or an individual competition. It may be called something different in different sports, but it is still a huddle. Before the game begins, before you go out and do anything, you have a meeting. The team gets together, the coach gives an inspirational speech, and you center yourself.

Think of Havdalah as the huddle before we begin the week. We gather the team together and have a moment before everyone heads their separate ways. We use three simple items to make the huddle interesting. The candle, the wine and the spices.

First, a Havdalah candle, which is a braided candle that can be purchased or made.

This time can be spent with others or by yourself, but usually there is no talking once you light the Havdalah candle. The candle is lit, you all stand, and you reflect on

"If we lived at the North Pole, would we only have one Havdalah a year?"

the week that has passed and think about what's coming up this week.

Second, it wouldn't be a Jewish ceremony without wine! Lift the glass and say the blessing over the wine if you know it, or you can say your own blessing. Perhaps, "Thank you God for the wine that makes the heart glad" before enjoying a sip.

The third item is a collection of spices. Make a blend of choice and put them in a jar or dish. Smell the spices. Now, look at the flame and thank God for the light in your life. Put out the candle and either think about or discuss what's happening the coming week, what you are looking forward to, and what you are worried about.

It's just like that huddle before the game. Review past plays and use that knowledge to plan the next one. That is why you gather for Havdalah: to compare notes, check in, and inform each other of what is coming up so you are prepared to face the week ahead.

That's Havdalah!

13
AS WE SAY IN HEBREW

SPRINKLE IN SOME HEBREW to up your Jewish. You are likely already saying "Oy Vey" or "Vey ist Meir," but those are negative Yiddish expressions. In this chapter, let's introduce a little positive Hebrew into your life. Here are some other words you can use that can incorporate Jewish culture into your life.

Rather than falling back on the time-honored "Oy Vey," you would be better served by saying "Baruch Hashem," which literally means "Blessed is God" but is used to mean, "Thank God!" In order to stop focusing on the negative aspects of every situation, stop using an expression of worry. Otherwise you might just miss out on something that could turn out to be good.

After attending a party that did not live up to your expectations, if your first reaction is to say "Oy Vey, poor me, this was a mistake." Was it? Perhaps you missed out on the pleasure and fun because you already judged that being there was a mistake. Instead say "Baruch Hashem. Thank God for exposing me to a potentially good time."

You have likely heard your parents and grandparents use any number of expressions, some you have incorporated into your lexicon while others are long forgotten. It's time to say, "I remember that expression!"

"Check out Lefty's scribbles."

It may not have fit into your life when you were 13, but it fits now.

Try saying "Gam Zeh L'Tova,' or, "This also is for good." Too often we dig down and try to find all the awful, bad, and terrible in the situation. But if you use the expression "Gam Zeh L'Tova," you admit that you might not fully understand what's going on, but in the end, it's going to be OK. Remember: when you find yourself in an uncomfortable or unpleasant situation, your thinking and perception of what is going on can make things worse.

Before you undertake a new project or activity, you'll want to say "B'Ezrat HaShem," which means "With God's help" or "God will help me." It's always nice to have God on your side. So, why not ask God for help? God does not cause things to happen nor does God mess up your life. It's not about predestination or things being determined, it is about free will. You may be doing something that you have never done before. However, "B'Ezrat HaShem," with God's help, you can do this.

"B'Hatz l'cha," means "may you be successful in this new endeavor you are undertaking." If someone you know is starting or in the middle of a difficult project say to them "B'Hatz l'cha," which is more than simply saying good luck, you're saying, "B'Hatz l'cha, I wish you good fortune."

Once your friend's project is finished, say "Yasher Koach," which means, "you did a great job, and congratulations on your success."

14
THE RABBI BLOCK CHALLENGE

DO YOU FEEL LIKE BEING CHALLENGED? You may have heard it before in different phrasing because many cultures and religions embrace this concept. "Don't do anything to another person that you would not want done to you." Grab a coin. One side represents how you want others to treat you, and the other side represents how you don't want people to treat you.

OK, so how does this work exactly? You are going to pause for a moment before you do anything or say anything and think, "Would I want that said or done to me?" If the answer is no, then don't do it. So, there, you have my challenge.

If somebody cuts you off on the Beltway or Route 66, you might ordinarily try and speed ahead, get in front of them, and cut them off in response. But you didn't like it done to you, so why are you going to do it to someone else? Remember the challenge.

In personal interactions, keep this challenge in mind. If someone says or does something to you that you don't like, stop. Say to yourself 'I don't think they're practicing the Rabbi Block challenge. I think they are being selfish.' Give them a pass on this one. You are not going to do or say it back because you wouldn't like it done to you.

The other side of the coin is the assumption that if you do something nice for someone, you're hoping that they will do nice things for you. I challenge you to rid yourself of these assumptions, because there is no guarantee of reciprocity.

Rather, think of it as a plus, a bonus for all of us, and a way to get around a lot of the nonsense that's going on in politics, religions, and in our families. Just stop and remember the challenge at each personal interaction.

One quick note: there is no scorekeeping, no punishment, and no physical reward to this challenge. Just watch and see how other people treat you after you have done this for a while.

You will be gratified by the results.

15
CAN'T STOP KVETCHING

KVETCHING, IS VERY JEWISH. Complaining may be one of the easiest ways to be Jewish because so often we complain without even thinking. Maybe you are already complaining about what you are reading! Kvetching comes naturally, but in Judaism, it is an art. Anyone can be a complainer, but a Jewish complaint has class and style.

Don't be seduced by those who tell you that kvetching won't make you happy. Or that you should be grateful and stop complaining. Stoics are the least happy people in the known universe and they are no fun to be around!

My grandmother would kvetch about me whenever the opportunity would arise. "My grandson Chiam is such a disappointment, he could have become a doctor! He could have become a lawyer. But, no, he had to become a Rabbi! What kind of a job is that for a Jewish boy?!" Now is not the time to hold back, kvetch about the things that you see around you, with being Jewish, and with this book.

Lets say your in-laws, best friend, crazy uncle Kenny, or anyone close to you gives you two really nice pictures, both of which you like. Knowing that they are coming over to visit you decide to hang one up so that it is

*"Please ask the chef if he could cook another steak, this time
one from a cow that he didn't have a grudge against."*

prominent. As soon as they see the picture they kvetch, "What's the matter; you didn't like the other one I gave you?"

Don't just simply blurt something out. Whenever you see something, hear something, taste something, make a complaint. But be elegant and perhaps make it humorous, and in all cases, make it entertaining because we want to kvetch.

One of the things that you're taught in the military is that when one of the troops in the squad stops complaining, that's when you know there's trouble. Because as long as the troops are complaining, they are interested in the activity and may want to make it better. This is true for you as well: You become a deserter or a quitter the moment you stop kvetching.

Once you start to practice kvetching, you may find it has an unexpected benefit. It's a bonding experience when you start kvetching. Try it; start kvetching and everyone around joins in complaining. Now everyone has bonded.

Hard to believe what a great experience can come out of complaining about the food you are eating, your parents, the government, your work, your partner, your Rabbi, the person who gave you this book, and more objects of kvetching are all around you! Don't miss an opportunity to utter an elegant, entertaining, or humorous complaint.

Even now: "You don't have time to call your mother, because you're reading a book written by some Rabbi?!"

"Either your priorities have shifted reasonable goals to unattainable expectations, or you're just plain messuganah."

16
SPRITZ SOME YIDDISH

YIDDISH IS PERFECT for describing the behavior of the people around you. Don't be quick to call everyone meshugganah, or crazy, because you have many other choices.

Perhaps they are being real nudniks, begging, staring, and making snide remarks so that you can't get any work done (that's the definition of a nudnik.) Furthermore, nudnik is not an inappropriate word, so your mother wouldn't wash your mouth out with soap for saying it. Nudnik describes a behavior, and speaking of ways to describe someone's behavior, being a vilde chaya means a person acting like a wild animal.

It is often used to describe when someone is running around causing havoc and distracting you. When this happens, feel free to shout it out, "Stop acting like a vilde chaya!" Note that expression is commonly directed at children, so when you say it to an adult it is a double insult!

If meshugganah is not yet your favorite expression, it will be, just don't ignore a whole range of other words in Yiddish that refer to someone's mental state. A meshugganah is someone whose language or behavior is a little bit crazy. You can probably recall many times when it would have been appropriate to say to someone, "Stop acting like a meshugganah." Or perhaps you have even asked yourself, "Am I acting like a meshugganah?"

Just remember that these Yiddish words describe behaviors, not one's mental state.

In contrast, if you call someone a mamzer you are referring to who they are and their character. The word mamzar is reserved for someone whose behavior is despicable, not cute or funny. Someone can be a nudnik, a vilde chaya, or a little meshuggadach and be crazy around the edges. But we use the word mumzar with intention to describe a mean-spirited person who acts maliciously without concern for anyone else.

So, every now and again, try out one of those words and see if you feel just a little bit more Jewish.

17
HONORING YAHRZEIT

YOU CAN BE JEWISH BY OBSERVING the anniversary
of a loved one's death. Since this is done once a year it is
called a Yahrzeit (literally, "year time," or anniversary).
We observe by lighting a candle that burns for 24 hours.

There are Yahrzeit candles available at major
supermarkets and online. However, the candle itself is
but a symbol. The choice of candle is not important,
because the point of lighting it is to help us remember.

In many religions and cultures, the birthday of
someone who died is observed and remembered, as is
their anniversary. We hear, "Oh, this would've been great
grandpa's 109th birthday," or "This would have been
their 80th anniversary." In contrast, Judaism focuses
on the date an individual passed. So why do we do it
this way?

The answer lies in the Talmud. One Rabbi said, "Which
is better: the day of birth or the day of death?" And since
the room was filled with Rabbis, the discussion went on
for hours! As we read the text, we watch the discussion
evolving and very slowly the Rabbis hone in on the
day of death as a day that you should use to focus on a
person's life, observe what they did, and remember them.
The Rabbis use the analogy of a ship; when a ship leaves

"He would have wanted it this way."

port it may crash, it may sink, or it will arrive safely with its cargo intact. We have no idea. They likened that idea to the day of birth. When someone is born you don't know anything about what their life will be like.

However, after someone's life unfolds, you know about the person, what they did, and what they didn't do. You know how they are to be remembered. The Rabbis concluded that we need an observance when someone dies because that's when we know the end of the story. We want to be able to say this person lived, this was their journey, and this was their life.

The date someone died is the day that their life came to an end. The ship returned home, whether with or without its cargo, having had either a successful or unsuccessful trip. We are not here to judge anything. We acknowledge that the person's life came to an end on that date, and we remember their life on the day that they died by lighting a candle.

*"All the tests came back negative. Whatever you're feeling,
it must all be in your head."*

18
SEEK IMMORTALITY

INCREDIBLE AND BEAUTIFUL PICTURES of our universe have come in from the James Webb telescope. Whenever I see one of the photographs of a beautiful star field it reminds me of a painting by Vincent van Gogh titled *Starry Starry Night.* He is immortalized by his paintings. I didn't realize until the other day that cartoonist Joe Sutliff doesn't sign a lot of his works. Thus, he is missing out on an opportunity, because in Judaism, immortality lies in what we leave behind.

So, create your own immortality. Leaving behind belongings like furniture, outdated electronics, your bell bottoms, and Nehru jackets will not make you immortal. Perhaps you'll instead be remembered for having bad taste, though... The goal is to leave behind your name associated with the good deeds you have done.

If you have the resources to do so, have a hospital wing named after you, a room in the library, the music room at your school, or a showcase outside the gym housing awards and trophies of student-athletes. If you love music, God willing your donation can secure a concert or practice hall named after you, a fund or foundation that buys or rents instruments to students, a display case in your Temple, or even a shelf full of books. When people look up and see your name they will remember you for the good you have done. In these ways, you'll be immortal.

Do you remember a teacher who influenced you, or a doctor, or neighbor who was kind to you and made an impression? Your immortality lies in being like them. It can be as simple as getting a kid's kite out of a tree, or any praiseworthy action. Reflect on people that you remember and why, then use their actions as your model, for they have Jewish immortality.

Be kind and perform acts of kindness so people will attach your name to something good. Imagine you're talking with someone when all of the sudden a teacher, a leader, or a friend comes into your mind. You remember them because of the good you associate with their name. In the same way, you want your name to be remembered for a blessing, just as you remember someone's name for a blessing.

19
HONOR THE OLD AND THE WISE

HONORING THE OLD AND THE WISE (someone like Yours Truly, for example) is another way you can be Jewish. According to the Book of Leviticus, we are told to "honor the old and the wise" in order to be happy and prosper in life. So, what is it about being old and wise that requires you to respect us, besides the fact that we lasted as long as we have? By showing how you treat the seniors among you, you are showing how you want to be treated. The wise are your role models, your moral compass, and they reflect the way you want to be viewed in your old age.

Keep in mind that wisdom doesn't come automatically with age. One can be an old fool, just as you can be wise beyond your years. The Torah doesn't link age and wisdom; they are two separate categories.

We want to honor someone who has both knowledge and wisdom. Usually, knowledge is acquired as you age. You see more, you do more, and you experience things differently.

How does honoring seniors apply to you? How society treats its seniors is a measure of its values. Nobody wants to be thrown away and dismissed as they age. In order to avoid this, simply treat others as you would like to be

"Avoid hangnails.'

treated in the years to come. Perhaps you are in a position to offer a job to two candidates and the only difference is age. Put aside the age difference and judge each candidate based on qualifications.

Honor the old and the wise. The Torah recognizes that those who have experienced a lot of life are a kind of living library, and the collective memory of a society. Honoring them honors your country and society as they'll become your personal, living library.

20
HAVE A NOSH

I'M ALWAYS READY FOR A NICE NOSH, aren't you?
A nosh is something you eat when you are not having a
meal. As Bubbe (grandmother) always said, "you should
never go to a meal hungry!" Besides, what's more Jewish
than eating? You might want to allow extra time for this
nice Jewish act.

Let's talk about some Jewish foods. Nosh once a week,
once a month, or whenever! The easy choice is bagels
because they are the first Jewish food that comes to mind.
One can get a bagel at McDonald's or Panera Bread, but
unfortunately, they're really not decent bagels.

Perhaps you'd like to try a few Jewish foods you've
never heard of! Perhaps a knish, some blintzes, Shav or
borsht? Better yet, talk to your mother, your grandmother,
Bubbe, Zadie, uncle, or aunt, and ask them for a list of
their favorite Jewish foods. Get the recipes. This way,
your source for Jewish food won't be Rabbi Block. Rather,
it is going to be your own family.

Find the oldest member of your family, your friends,
family, or anybody, really, You want to enlarge your scope
to make this a family affair and create something that
connects you with your family and friends. You might
be pleasantly surprised that talking about Jewish food

"I made your favorite—chicken with fourteen kinds of kuggle."

connects you with the old members of your own family. And that, in itself, is well worth your time.

I guarantee that whatever your family is serving you will enjoy. You might develop a taste for gefilte fish, lox, herring, or whitefish. Besides, a bagel with a shmear of cream cheese goes great with a salty fish. And please, find a bakery that makes "real" bagels to discover what a bagel should taste like!

21
THE HAPPY MONTH

BEING JEWISH IS EASY, simple, and quick, but perhaps this is the easiest, simplest, and quickest way to be Jewish. During the month of Adar, we are required to be happy, because Adar is the happy month. We are commanded, no required to rejoice and have a good time during the month of Adar.

The Hebrew calendar is a solar-corrected lunar calendar, so holidays can shift as much as 30 days in relation to the secular calendar. When is the month of Adar exactly? It can fall as early as the middle of February or as late as the middle of March, sometimes it's around Valentine's Day and other times, it's around Saint Patrick's Day.

We can choose to be happy or unhappy 11 months of the year, but it's a commandment to be happy during the month of Adar. We can even save up all our happiness for one month and be miserable the other 11 months. But Judaism singles out the month of Adar as the happy month. The reason is that the holiday of Purim falls during the month of Adar.

On the holiday of Purim, we dress up in costumes, drink, and have all kinds of fun activities. One of the classic activities is the "Purim Shpiel," a comic play that tells the Purim story. Participate in the mitzvah of hearing

the Book of Esther read aloud. When the names of the heroes, Esther and Mordechai, are read, we cheer, and when the name of the villain Haman is read, we boo. Many of those attending will be in costume.

Happiness doesn't depend on hearing the Book of Esther, however. Take your dog out for a walk, eat your favorite dessert, read a book—do things that make you smile. Do happy things with your friends, be happy more than once, be happy for 30 seconds, and, in a couple of days, be happy for 30 seconds again. You can be happy the whole month, the whole year, but at minimum, be happy for 30 seconds.

Needless to say, if reading this book makes you happy, keep reading and keep smiling. If you'd like you can send me an email about what you did for 30 seconds that made you happy.

22
ENJOY LIFE

L'CHIAM, "TO LIFE!" Life is good when you enjoy what
you're doing, L'Chiam! Enjoy everything God created
because everything God created is good. Sometimes
as humans we go overboard, lose track, or we fail to do
things in moderation. Even the most pleasurable
activities in life—when taken to the extreme—are no
longer pleasurable.

"T.G.I.F.!!!"

For example, it is written in the Book of Psalms and the Book of Proverbs, and others that wine makes the heart glad. Nowhere does it say not to drink. Yet it does say not to become intoxicated or drunk. Never drink to the point that you don't know what you're doing.

Jewish values support moderation. There are some things and activities where no amount is healthy which means we should stay away from them. They're off the table. I started with alcohol or wine because, in moderation, it is OK to party to dance to sing to have a good time. All of this is part of saying L'chaim, to life, so go ahead and enjoy.

That is what this whole being Jewish thing means. Enjoy what God has given, created, and presented to you, and practice moderation in all you do. L'chiam!

23
MAKE A MITZVAH

MANY INTERPRET THE WORD MITZVAH as doing a good deed. That is the simple explanation, but not the word's only meaning. Examples of doing a mitzvah might be donating to a food bank, taking out the garbage, or emptying the dishwasher. But the word mitzvah means one of the 613 Commandments in the Torah. You are probably thinking that there are only ten commandments, right? The Ten Commandments in Judaism are called the ten utterances, and they are just ten of the 613. A reasonable person could say that 613 is far too many and feel overwhelmed.

Broken down there are 77 positive and 194 negative commandments that can be observed today, of which 26 commands apply only within the Land of Israel, and only after the Messiah has come. Many of the remaining commandments apply to farming or other narrow situations. We observe many of the rest without even realizing it because they are included in the legal system or as part of our culture.

So, if we want to do a mitzvah, does this mean we have to look up the 613 commandments and then figure out which ones apply today? Why not just start with the first ten?

The first commandment given is to be fruitful and multiply; to fill the earth with children. If you are married you can fulfill it immediately. If not, it will have to wait until you are married. That's because this commandment applies to a married couple —not to sowing your wild oats. Try looking at your spouse and saying you'd like to fulfill one of God's commandments. It's a pretty solid opening line…

"*My apologies, but wait... I think I have an app for this.*"

24
DERECH ERETZ;
POLITENESS COUNTS

I DON'T WANT TO BE RUDE, but it's time to start being polite. Derech eretz means to be polite and courteous. When we hear the words derech eretz we might hear our mother, grandmother, grandfather, or father.

Derech eretz is a concept independent of how people will think of you. It's about how you should behave in society. Whether you're alone at home or in a hotel room, you might not be so concerned about being polite. However, in public, once you are with other people, that's when you want to pay close attention to derech eretz. Are you being polite? Did you say "please" and "thank you," smile, and acknowledge other people's presence and what they have to say?

You might be thinking that Derech Eretz refers to knowing which fork to use for the salad versus the fish course, or why we need all those glasses. That is social etiquette, which applies to specific social settings.

What you will discover is if you are polite even some of the most impolite, obnoxious people will soon become polite in response. They will likely realize that they are being rude to you. Derech eretz is the default; being rude and obnoxious is a choice.

Thank you for taking the time to consider the benefits that derech eretz offers. If you want, you can always send me an email with your questions about which fork to use though.

25
DON'T PASS OVER PASSOVER

IN THE SPRING, it's time to think about Passover and the Seder. I know what you're thinking: Passover takes days or even months to prepare, and the Seder itself lasts for hours. Maybe you're thinking this is going to be a real challenge for only 30 seconds. While you probably have family and friends who spend days, weeks, or months getting ready for Passover, that prep is optional. You can certainly start preparing an elaborate Passover meal at any time, getting things ready, pre-cooking and putting stuff in the freezer. However, Passover is a holiday to celebrate freedom, with the Seder meal as a vehicle, not the goal.

The word seder means "order." It's an ordered meal that reminds us of the value of freedom. That's Passover in a nutshell. Often people get scared off because they think that the only way to observe the Passover is with some elaborate, boring, overwhelming meal. But a five-minute Seder is enough. Cut down on the preparation and simply invite family and friends over for a nice meal.

The seder guides us through the story of the exodus from Egypt. There are 15 elements in the Passover Seder, which could take as little as five minutes to go over. The whole purpose of the Seder is to mention these elements

*"...and let's all thank Timmy for adding some
realism to the Seder."*

and that's it; all the rest is commentary, discussion, or stories. Maybe you remember your grandparents, great-grandparents, or your parents taking hours to complete the Seder. While it certainly can take hours, a longer version is not more praiseworthy. What is praiseworthy is to mention each of the elements, to look at each other, and say freedom is important. It is easy and simple to go on line and find the elements needed for a Seder. People have shared Seders online that range from 5 minutes to several hours and everything in between.

There you have it, a five-minute Seder! Now you can look forward to your Seder instead of dreading it. Embrace the 15 elements and their symbolism and not obsess over the food. Have the Seder catered or use takeaway from a supermarket. Just don't lose sight of the fact that it's about celebrating freedom, reminding ourselves and each other of what it was like being a slave in Egypt.

"...and the Passover alternative, with or without water."

26
ESCHEW CHAMETZ

UNFORTUNATELY, your leftover Mardi Gras pretzels are chametz so you'll need to save them for after Passover. When Passover begins you won't be able to eat any chametz. During Passover, you are asked to stay away from products that have yeast or leavening in them, wheat products, or anything that could rise by getting wet. The rules about leavening are as extensive as everything is in Judaism. My goal here is to simplify what it means to observe the Passover: stay away from products that have yeast and those that could rise. These are generally bread products or cookies or crackers.

To simplify further, if you stick to vegetables, you don't have to worry about chametz, because they don't have any leavening in them. You are welcome to eat all kinds of grains, including rice. There's a misconception that rice was prohibited, but that's over now so you can eat rice during Passover.

The holiday of Passover observes the exodus from Egypt. The Israelites, having been freed from slavery, are heading out on the journey towards the Promised Land. During Passover week you are going to refrain from eating bread, plain and simple. Don't be concerned with all the complicated rules, what your grandmother said, or what other people do, because that can become much too complicated. This is not what being Jewish is about.

Perhaps simply pick something to refrain from eating during Passover. Not something random, though. Choose something that has leavening in it, so that it has risen. Maybe you'll choose cake, cookies, or a favorite bread. The idea is to remind yourself of the Exodus and the importance of freedom. I would also add you are not required to eat matzah all week long. Matzah is eaten only during the Seder; the other times it is voluntary.

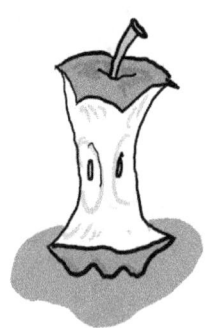

27
THREE VERSES

NOW THAT WE'VE BEEN TALKING a lot about the Torah and the Bible, and about spirituality, I want to bring up the physical for a second. Given that a good amount of reading material is available online, do we need to have a copy of the Torah in our houses? Is it easier or better? I think it's very important to have a copy of the Scriptures. Maybe you have a family Bible at home, or a copy that was given to you or one of your children at a b'nai mitzvah.

"If Moses had turned left at Goshen, we'd have all that oil."

Again, don't get bogged down in a specific translation or anything like that. What is important is to have a copy of the Torah. It's both symbolic and you may want to refer to it. For example, you may hear something in a movie or TV show when someone quotes Torah and you might want to see what comes before or what comes after what is being read.

Want to do more? Set up a schedule and decide to read three verses every day, every other day, once a month, or once a week, starting with Genesis. Or if you'd like to be mystical, choose a book from the Torah: Genesis, Exodus, Numbers, Leviticus, or Deuteronomy and use your birthday to select the chapter and verse. Perhaps read the Book of Psalms, the Book of Proverbs, or just open a page at random. Use an anniversary date or a Yahrzeit date (the date of someone's death), all of these are mystical ways to tease out some words of wisdom, and turn it into something important.

Give it a try; pick up yours and see what you can find.

28
BLESS THE CHILDREN

IN TRADITIONAL JUDAISM, one blesses the children every Sabbath. Traditionally you would light the candles and then bless the children, recite the blessing for the bread and the wine, and then have a Sabbath meal. That is the traditional format, so if that works for your family, do that. Perhaps your family gathers to eat on Friday night without lighting candles or reciting any blessings. Why don't you add in blessing the children?

For everything in Judaism, there is a proscribed blessing. The traditional blessings refer to biblical people and tribes. I have nothing against the tribes, the matriarchs or patriarchs.

Start by choosing someone you would like your child to emulate. Maybe grandparents or great-grandparents. Maybe a sports figure, an actress or an actor, a teacher, or a neighbor. Sometimes you put your hands on the heads of your children. Sometimes you hug your children. Perhaps a group hug. Try out different procedures to see what feels right. After all, blessing your children every week is what is Jewish instead of the recitation of specific words.

It is even more important to bless your children when they become teenagers who roll their eyes or glare at you.

"You can bless'em, but first you'll have to catch 'em!"

This is an appropriate time to change the blessing. When your kids are little, cute, and cuddly, there are certain people that you may want to be like. But when they get to be teenagers you may want it to reinforce their sports or other activities. You can pick a figure who excels at the same sport that your children practice. It can be someone from baseball, basketball, rugby, or any sport. And you can say "May you become like... and be blessed with the same attributes and skills that they are blessed with". The blessing becomes the perfect occasion to acknowledge and validate their interests.

29
RADICAL AMAZEMENT

BEING AMAZED BY WHAT YOU SEE around you is very Jewish. Rabbi Abraham Joshua Heschel talked and wrote about radical amazement—perfect for 30 seconds. It's easy, and simple; you become closer to God by becoming amazed by what God created.

Too often we are in a hurry. In the process, Heschel taught, you are missing a connection with God. Radical amazement causes happiness. You don't need to change your routine, just be amazed.

Watch a young child if you want to witness radical amazement. Children are not just surprised, not just appreciative, but they are thrilled by every little thing, which brings them closer to God. The more we distance ourselves from our feelings and emotions of amazement, the further we drift from God.

There is so much around you that you miss because your mind is somewhere else.

Be amazed at how your fingers work. Be amazed at the microwave. Heschel said to take off your blinders and start allowing yourself to see the area around you, the universe around you. Make radical amazement a part of your daily drill. The next time you visit the supermarket, walk down the cereal aisle. Look left and right; it's

"We may never know what makes them gather like that... it's just one of those mysteries of nature."

amazing the number of breakfast cereals that exist.

This is how you connect to God— by being radically amazed by everything around you.

30
KEEP THE FAITH...OR NOT

YOU ARE NOT REQUIRED to find a nice Jewish boy or girl for yourself, your son, or your daughter. As soon as you think there's only one thing that'll make you or your children happy, you are dooming the relationship. After all, what is dating about anyway? Dating is about having experiences that help you develop your own standards for a partner. I am saying that it's OK to date someone of a different religion than yours.

Think of dating as going into the supermarket and heading to the cereal aisle. There are innumerable boxes of cereal, with each containing different amounts of sugar, different grains, and blends. all different. In and of themselves none are better, none are worse. The cereals are there for your choosing. That is how to view dating. You are walking down the aisle and you are looking for a partner. What are your criteria?

In the end, you are going to need to taste the cereal to see if you like it. It's the same with dating. You need to be with a variety of individuals to find the fit that is right for you.

After dating, you may decide that certain personality types are not compatible with you. You may decide that it's not a specific religion that creates a problem, but how

*"Your mother and I don't mind, but what will
the rest of the family think?*

they view their religion. In any case, you don't want
to eliminate someone because they're not Jewish. That
would be a mistake. Instead, see how you feel about the
person, discover how the relationship develops, and then
you'll find out if he or she is right for you.

31
CIRCUMCISION

CIRCUMCISION ONLY TAKES about 30 seconds. I will spare you the myriad of jokes on the subject. Reform Judaism does not require circumcision to be performed by an orthodox specialist (mohel) on the 8th day, but that doesn't mean you can't have your son circumcised on the 8th day by a mohel. It does mean that you should consider the Reform movement's study and review of the meaning of circumcision. The medical procedure can be done in the hospital at birth and the covenant/naming ceremony can take place later.

What I'm going to be telling you is not my idea. It's not new. It comes out of Reform Judaism with a lot of research and a lot of documentation. The Reform movement recognized that circumcision was two processes, two things were happening. One is a medical procedure: the circumcision. The other is a naming ceremony that brings your son into the covenant of Israel and gives him a Hebrew name. Two separate things are happening, so the Reform movement argues and advocates that you should have a choice.

A Brit Mila, translates to the covenant of circumcision, so one could even separate the medical procedure from the covenant ceremony. According to Reform Judaism,

"He says he wants to be a Mohel someday."

it a circumcision in the hospital is just as Jewish as having your son circumcised by a mohel, in your home on the eighth day. If you're concerned about a medical procedure being done outside a hospital, the covenant ceremony can happen afterward, in the home. After all, we bring our daughters into the covenant of Israel with a ceremony without circumcision.

The Reform movement looked at the passages in the Torah and concluded that for a particular time and place, they made sense. Like so many other injunctions in the Torah, they cannot be taken literally and applied for all time. Circumcision belongs in a hospital, you bring your son into the community of Israel through a ceremony. What was appropriate thousands of years ago is not appropriate now. Your sons and daughters become Jewish not by a medical procedure, but with an appropriate ceremony.

32
BE OPEN TO NEW IDEAS

I AM WATCHING A BEAUTIFUL SUNSET over the golf course. I had a great round today because the other three in my foursome gave me some new ideas. Being open to new ideas is one of the keys to Jewish survival. Whenever you are presented with a new idea, give yourself 30 seconds before you ignore it. No matter how long you have been playing golf, your game can always be improved.

What is it about new ideas that you cringe when you hear them? I know one of the downfalls of almost all religions seems to be that they don't want to hear a different opinion, a new direction, or a challenge to the way things have been done. It's not just religions that are afraid of new ideas; governments, societies, or even countries fear change. When it comes to steering away from new ideas, nobody is immune.

Look at the historic record any time a religion or society closes itself off from change or new ideas: we see its downfall. Staying open to new ideas is something that's both extremely easy and difficult at the same time. Being open and willing to listen to someone else instead of having a knee-jerk reaction is a great starting point.

When the Reform movement began, there were a lot of

"No, I don't know how far we want to go out.
Is that a problem?"

new ideas. When we look back, we realize that some of these ideas didn't work, so they fell away. It's the constant change and evolution that helps keep Judaism alive.

While you're listening to someone else you don't start thinking of a response or how to answer them. More often than not you say something at that moment you are no longer listening to someone else. You are formulating a rebuttal an argument or an answer, so what I'm asking you is to resist that urge. Stop and listen to the other person. You are not agreeing or disagreeing just because you're listening. After you listen to the idea why not just say wait a minute for something I'd like to talk to you again about that subject, but not right now I want to go online and look some things up.

By taking 30 seconds to listen and be open while another person is talking, you may find you actually agree with them, at least partially.

"In my day we had to download our own apps to have fun!"

33
NEGOTIATE NOSTALGIA

REMEMBER SITTING in your grandma's kitchen having fond memories of growing up Jewish. And fond memories of growing up Jewish are a great way to be Jewish in 30 seconds. The way things used to be when you were young, makes classic Jewish family memories. Trips down memory lane are fun and satisfying, as they mean you are reliving your Judaism.

Nostalgia is a good thing as long as we recognize that they are memories and just that. We often re-create many of our memories, making them into what we would like them to be, based on books, movies, and TV shows. This can create a romanticized past, which is fine as long as we acknowledge that it is just that, a past that never really happened.

Take a great family Seder, for example. Perhaps you want to re-create what your grandfather did at his Seders because he knew what it meant to be Jewish. Just consider that what you are recreating may never have existed. Perhaps you should hire some Hollywood writers and actors to create that kind of Seder!

Please leave nostalgia where it belongs—as a fond memory. Don't make your nostalgic memories the standard for your Judaism today. Your Jewishness today is a Judaism that you are creating here and now.

That said, it's still a great idea to pull things from your memory now and then to help create your Jewish future. How did your grandmother and grandfather, your Bubbie and Zadie, lead the Seder? What did they add? What did they gloss over? How did they entertain you? Just be careful that what they did doesn't become the standard that you judge how Jewish you are today. We go to the past for inspiration, and then bring what we find into the present.

After all, our grandparents and great-grandparents were Jewish in the 18th and 19th centuries and everything was different then. The past is the place that we go to help create observances that are meaningful to us so that our Judaism becomes 21st-century Judaism.

34
LIVING WITHIN YOUR MEANS

JUDAISM TEACHES THAT in order to be happy, be content with what you have at this moment. Being content with your income is no easy task. Nearly everybody wishes they had a little bit more, and perhaps you are even one of them. How many people do you know who are content with the status quo?

The teaching doesn't mean you don't ask for a raise or look for another job that earns more money. Judaism teaches us to be satisfied where we are presently. Getting another job and moving up the corporate ladder is very, very Jewish as long as we are content where we are. If we're always chasing the next promotion in order to be happy, the promotion was never going to bring us happiness.

Judaism teaches moderation; that the middle leads to happiness and contentment. That's why the basic teaching is "who is content, he who is happy with what that person has". So, focus on what you have and ask yourself why you are not content with that. Obviously there will always be a bigger house or a more impressive car. Just be sure to stop and thank God for what we have.

Don't let your present-day happiness be ruined by focusing on future acquisitions. Instead, be content with

"A glass of your finest tap water and some ketchup if you please, and bring a bowl for my faithful companion."

where you are. Enjoy what you have while keeping an eye open for a promotion, raise, or another job with more money. Your happiness and your family's happiness doesn't depend on what you don't have, but rather what you do.

35
DON'T OBSERVE, EMBRACE

THIS SOUNDS ODD coming from a Rabbi, but I'm serious: Embrace, don't practice. Embrace Judaism in 30 seconds a day. Embrace the rituals you choose to do. Looking back on the previous chapters, we should embrace having a Sabbath meal, and embrace blessing our children. We shouldn't focus on how to do it, the rules, or whether we are doing it right. There is no punishment if we do the ritual wrong, nor is there a reward for doing them correctly.

If all we're doing is putting the pieces together, we're putting unnecessary pressure and worry on ourselves. What's more, when we worry about performing the ritual exactly, we are not in the moment. Radical amazement means being in the moment and not worrying about being perfect. You'll be amazed by what happens when you embrace the moment and embrace each of the things that we choose to do Jewishly. We each have a spiritual path—find what works for you.

Perhaps you have turned away from Judaism because too many people out there are promoting their way rather than saying, "embrace the commandments, embrace the ritual, and don't be petty." When God said, "Love your neighbor as yourself," He wanted you to embrace the

"Our teacher said we had to learn how to embrace art."

idea of loving your neighbor as yourself and embrace
the Golden Rule.

36
SPEND MORE THAN
THIRTY SECONDS

YOU HAVE COME TO THE 36TH CHAPTER of "How to be Jewish in 30 Seconds." 36 is a multiple of 18, which is the numerical value of the Hebrew word for life: chai. This one might take you a little bit longer than 30 seconds, so relax, grab your favorite beverage, and continue reading…

Whether it's every day or once a month, it is up to you to decide how much you are going to do and how often. Don't let yourself become overwhelmed by the totality of Judaism, all the rituals, and all the practices that are out there.

I selected 35 specific activities that could be done quickly and easily. In chapter 35 I talked specifically about embracing and living the practice rather than just going through the motions while checking things off.

You are currently reading chapter 36—double Chai. So how much do you want to live through Judaism? By now, you've had a chance to practice some different things. Do you want to do more? Do you want to embrace more Judaism every day? Do you want to expand the holiday observances you read about?

"Do you like it? CNN was having a tag sale."

Besides the Shabbat meal, you may want to dedicate the day, half the day, or any part of the day as a day off from everyday life. Perhaps a five-minute Seder was enjoyable so you want to do more. The holiday of Shavuot celebrates the giving of the Torah. Consider learning more Torah, reading more than a few lines on occasion.

Suppose you decide that being Jewish for 30 seconds is satisfying or even enjoyable! You'll feel content, and friends and family may start to notice things are going well for you. Consider expanding your practice to being Jewish in 60 seconds. The goal is to add meaning to your life and create a relationship with God. By embracing Judaism you are creating your own definition of God. Does observing Judaism for 30 seconds help unite you with God? Are you spiritually fulfilled? Perhaps you have discovered that you need a little bit more.

Take care and happy trails, wherever you are on your spiritual path.

Whether you embrace and practice for 30 seconds or 24 hours, Judaism will keep you company. And it's always nice to have company...

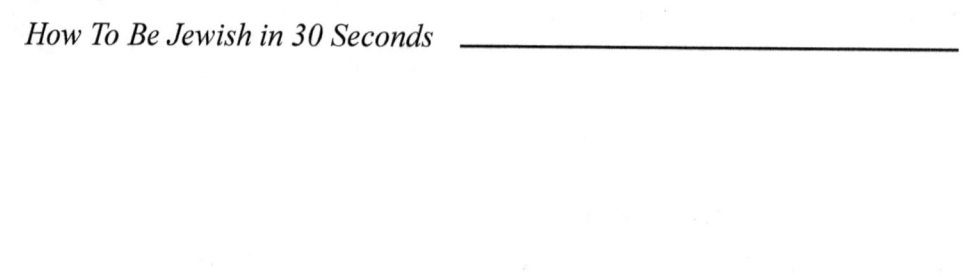

ACKNOWLEDGEMENTS

FIRST AND FOREMOST, I want to thank my cartoonist and partner, Joe Sutliff, who kept me on subject and edited out segments that were important and interesting, but not on topic. This book, just like our "The Rabbi and I" YouTube Channel and Podcast, is a truly a joint effort.

Writers are only as good as their editors. I am grateful to have two—my daughter Jenny Block and her best friend Rachel Pinn. They made my text a pleasure to read miraculously without changing content or meaning.

I want to thank the Boston College class of 1968. My undergraduate education taught me to think, to learn, and to teach. Critical thinking was woven into the curriculum. Having a basic classical education has helped me to make sense of current events and world politics.

I also owe a debt of gratitude to the Hebrew Union College-Jewish Institute of Religion Cincinnati Campus where I learned to value Judaism. I learned and practiced what I needed to become a teacher and a preacher.

A special thanks to Barbara Sutliff for making the text ascetically pleasing. Without her expertise, the book would look like it was reproduced on my old Smith Corona!

And, finally, thank you to Cole Tax Services of Rockville, MD. With their help, I have learned to run a small business. And, needless to say, I don't pay any more in taxes than I am required to pay.